The Best Retirement Guide
for Adults

Successful Techniques to Make Your
Money Last a Lifetime

Rebecca W. Anderson

Copyright 2023

Content

Introduction

Introduction

Save wisely, always!

Save money, maintain saving money, and stay committed to your goals.

If you're already saving money, whether it's for retirement or another objective, keep it up! You are aware that saving is a rewarding practice. If you're not saving, you should start now. Attempt to raise the amount you save each month, even if you have to start small. The figure below illustrates how saving earlier gives your money more time to grow. Prioritize retirement planning.

Make a plan, follow it, and set objectives. Never forget that it's never too early or late to start saving. Recognize the requirements for your retirement.

Retirement is costly. According to experts, in order to maintain your quality of life once you stop working, you would need between 70 and 90 percent of your preretirement income. Take responsibility for your financial future.

Planning ahead is the secret to a safe retirement. Begin by requesting For those close to retirement, Savings Fitness: Taking the Mystery Out of Retirement Planning is a guide to your money and your financial future. To order a copy, see the back panel.

Put money into your employer's retirement savings plan

Become a member and make the maximum contribution if your workplace offers a 401(k) plan or other retirement savings option. Automatic deductions make it simple, and your taxes will be reduced. Your employer might also contribute more. Compound interest and tax deferrals have a significant impact on the amount you will eventually amass.

Ask about your strategy. For instance, how much would you need to pay in order to receive the entire employer contribution, and how long would you need to participate in the plan in order to do so?

Study the pension plan offered by your work.

Check to determine if you are protected by the standard pension plan offered by your company, and learn how it operates. To determine the value of your benefit, get an individual benefit statement. Find out how your pension benefit may vary before changing jobs. Find out what advantages you might have from a prior workplace.

Ascertain whether you are eligible for benefits under your spouse's plan. Please inquire for further details. What to Know About Your Retirement Plan. For more information, go to the back panel.

Think about fundamentals for investing

Saving habits might be just as crucial as amount of money saved. Your retirement savings will depend significantly on inflation as well as the type of investments you make. Understand the investments made in your retirement account. Ask questions and become knowledgeable about your plan's investment possibilities. Place your savings in a variety of investments. You are more likely to lower risk and increase return by diversifying in this way.

Depending on a variety of variables, including your age, ambitions, and financial situation, your investment mix may alter over time. Financial stability and education go hand in hand.

Do not access your retirement funds.

You could lose tax advantages or incur fines if you withdraw your retirement funds now. You would also lose principle and interest.

If you move jobs, either keep your funds invested in your current retirement plan or transfer them to an IRA or the plan offered by your new company.

Request a plan from your workplace.

Encourage your employer to start a retirement plan if it doesn't already have one. Numerous options for saving plans are available. In order to benefit both you and your employer, your company may be able to set up a simple plan.

You can obtain a copy of Choosing a Retirement Solution for Your Small Business to learn more. For additional details, see the back panel.

Contribute funds to a retirement account, individual

An Individual Retirement Account (IRA) allows for annual contributions of up to $6,000; those 50 and older are eligible for higher contributions. You might also start with considerably less. Tax benefits are another feature of IRAs.

You can open either a regular IRA or a Roth IRA when you open an IRA. Depending on which option you choose, your contributions and withdrawals will have a different tax treatment. Inflation and the kind of IRA you select will also affect the after-tax value of your distribution. An easy way to save is through IRAs. You can arrange for money to be automatically taken out of your checking or savings account and placed into the IRA.

Discover your Social Security benefits.

The amount of pre-retirement income that Social Security retirement benefits replace for beneficiaries is typically 40%. You might be able to calculate your benefit by utilizing the retirement estimator on the Social Security Administration's website.

Visit their website or contact 1-800-772-1213 for additional details.

You'll need more information, even though these suggestions are meant to guide you. Take a look at the publications listed on the back panel. Speak with your employer, bank, union, or financial advisor. Ask questions, and then make sure you comprehend the responses.

Chapter 1

Your road to retirement starts right here.

There is still time to increase your savings before you retire. You still have time to increase your retirement funds if you're between the ages of 55 and 64. Having a sufficient amount of money saved can make all the difference, both financially and psychologically, whether you want to retire early, late, or never. Building out—or, if necessary, catching up—should be your main priority.

There is never a bad time to start saving, but the ten or so years before to retirement can be particularly important. By then, you'll probably have a very solid notion of when (or if) you want to retire, and even more crucially, you'll still have time to make modifications if necessary.

Consider these six tried-and-true retirement savings strategies if you find that you need to save more money.

1. Invest the most in your 401(k).

It's a good idea to increase your contributions right away if your employer offers a 401(k) or a comparable plan, such a 403(b) or 457, and you aren't already supporting yours to the maximum.

Such plans not only offer a simple, automatic way to invest, but they also allow you to postpone paying taxes on the income until you withdraw it in retirement.Since your peak earning years are most likely to be in your 50s and early 60s, you may also be in a higher marginal tax bracket now than you will be when you retire, which will result in a lower tax burden later on.

Of course, regular 401(k)s and other tax-advantaged plans are covered by this. If you decide to invest in a Roth 401(k) through your employer, you will pay taxes on your income at the time of contribution but will be able to take your funds tax-free in the future.

Each year, your plan's maximum contribution amount is raised to account for inflation. Anyone under the age of 50 will pay $22,500 in 2023. But if you're 50 or older, you can add a $7,500 catch-up payment for a total of $30,000 instead.

2. Review the allocations in your 401(k).

According to conventional financial wisdom, as you get older, you should invest more cautiously, placing more of your money in bonds and less in stocks. The thinking is that if your stocks fall in a protracted bear market, you won't have as many years for prices to rebound and you might have to sell at a loss.

Whether or not you should become more cautious depends on your risk tolerance and personal preferences, but few financial advisors would advise selling all of your stock assets and switching exclusively to bonds, regardless of your age. Bonds lack the growth potential that stocks provide. The key is to maintain a healthy level of diversification in both stocks and bonds while doing so in an age-appropriate way.

For instance, a cautious portfolio would be made up of 70 to 75 percent bonds, 15 to 20 percent stocks, and 5 to 15 percent in cash or cash equivalents, such as money-market funds. A portfolio that is relatively conservative might increase the stock portion to 35% to 40% and decrease the bond portion to 55% to 60%.

It's important to take a close look at your investment allocation if you're still contributing to the same mutual funds or other investments that you made in your 20s, 30s, or 40s in your 401(k). As you approach retirement age, you should consider whether you feel comfortable with that allocation.

Target-date funds are a convenient choice that many plans now provide; these funds automatically change their asset allocations as the year you intend to retire gets closer. Consider your options carefully as target-date funds may have higher costs.

3. You may want to add an IRA.

An individual retirement account (IRA) is an additional retirement investing option if your employer does not offer a 401(k) plan or if you have already funded yours to the maximum. In 2023, the most you can put into an IRA is $6,500, plus an additional $1,000 if you're 50 or older.

Even if their birthday occurs at the end of the year, people who turn 50 at the end of a calendar year are still eligible to make the full amount of yearly catch-up payments for that year.

Traditional and Roth IRAs are both available. You can deduct your contribution from your taxes in the year you make it if you donate to a traditional IRA. With a Roth IRA, you receive your tax break in the form of tax-free withdrawals at the other end.

The laws governing donation caps differ for the two categories as well.

standard IRAs

You can deduct the full amount of your conventional IRA contribution if neither you nor your spouse participate in a workplace retirement plan. Depending on your income and filing status and whether one of you is covered by a retirement plan, your contribution may be at least partially deductible.

A Roth IRA

As previously stated, Roth contributions are not tax deductible, regardless of your income or possession of a workplace retirement plan. On that sum of money, taxes will be paid that year.

But whether you can make a Roth contribution in the first place depends on your income. At the top of an income range, the permitted contribution is lowered in stages until it reaches zero. The figures are modified each year.

The income phase-out range for taxpayers contributing to a Roth IRA for the 2023 tax year is between $138,000 and $153,000 for singles and heads of household. The range is $218,000 to $228,000 for married couples filing jointly. It ranges between $0 and $10,000 for a married person filing a separate return.

Additionally, keep in mind that married couples who file their taxes jointly may frequently fund two IRAs through a spousal IRA, even if only one spouse has a paying job. The regulations are laid out in IRS Publication 590-A.

4. Be Aware of What You're Receiving

The additional retirement income streams you might realistically expect to have an impact on how aggressively you should save. In comparison to earlier in your career, you can acquire a far more accurate estimate if you're in your mid-50s or early 60s.

Old-fashioned Pensions

You ought to be getting an individual benefit statement at least once every three years if your present or former company has a defined-benefit pension plan. Additionally, you can ask the administrator of your plan for a copy once a year.

The statement should detail the rewards you've received and the date on which they become entirely yours (or "vested").

It's important to understand the formula used to determine your pension benefits. Numerous plans employ formulae that take into account pay and service history. Therefore, if you can, consider staying on the job longer to reap greater rewards.

Public Assistance

With ten years or more of Social Security contributions under your belt, you can use the Social Security Retirement Estimator to generate a customized estimate of your future monthly payments. If you keep working, your benefits can increase because they will be based on your 35 greatest years of earnings.

The benefits you receive will also differ based on when you begin receiving them. If you begin receiving benefits before reaching your "full" retirement age, which is presently 66 or 67 for those born after 1943, they would be permanently lowered from the amount you would receive if you waited until that age. To receive the greatest benefit, you can postpone taking Social Security until you are 70 years old.

To put it into perspective, the highest potential benefit—for someone who paid the maximum amount into the system each year starting at age 22 and waited until age 70 to begin collecting—would be $4,194 in 2022. In comparison, the average monthly retirement payment as of November 2022 is $1,691.53. The maximum benefit is $4,555 in 2023.

Additionally, bear in mind that if your total income is less than $25,000 for an individual or $32,000 for a couple, you will lose some of your Social Security payout to income taxes. Since 1984, Social Security benefits are taxed.1819

It's preferable to leave the money alone and allow it continue to grow, even though you may be able to withdraw money without penalty from your retirement plans as early as age 50 or 55 in some circumstances.

5. Do Not Use Your Retirement Savings

You can start taking withdrawals without incurring penalties from your IRAs and regular retirement plans after you reach age 5912. You can take a penalty-free withdrawal of your contributions from a Roth IRA at any age, but not any earnings.

For employees 55 and older (50 and over for some federal employees), there is also an IRS provision known as the Rule of 55 that waives the early-withdrawal penalty on retirement plan distributions. Because it's complicated, it's recommended to consult a financial or tax professional if you're thinking about utilizing it.

However, you shouldn't withdraw money simply because you can unless you really need it. The longer you keep your retirement savings untouched, the better off you'll probably be. However, if you were born between 1951 and 1959, you must start taking required minimum distributions at the age of 73, or 75 if you were born in 1960 or later. The prior age was 72, therefore this is an increase.

6. Avoid Ignoring Taxes

Last but not least, keep in mind that not all of the money you save for retirement is yours to keep. The IRS will impose taxes on withdrawals from traditional 401(k)-type plans and traditional IRAs at your ordinary income tax rate, not at the reduced capital gains tax rate.

Therefore, every $1,000 you remove will only provide you $780 if you are in the 22% tax rate, for example. You might want to make plans to keep more of your retirement money, such moving to a place with lower taxes.

Chapter 2
Family Relationships
How to support the person you care about without jeopardizing your retirement

When you are retired, you can take pleasure in your accomplishments and spend time with your loved ones. However, striking a balance between your desire to provide for your family and your financial objectives can be difficult. Following are some suggestions for providing for your loved ones without risking your retirement:

Schedule a Meeting With a Financial Counselor.
If a family member requests a loan, you could want to teach them about money instead. To learn more about setting up a budget, saving money, and making plans for the future, bring your family member to a consultation with a financial counselor. "Giving this opportunity for the wise counsel of a trusted advisor can pay off many times over and help build sound financial habits," claims Michele Lee Fine, head of Cornerstone Wealth Advisory in New York.

Send Out More Dinner Invitations
You can stay up to date on each other's lives and events by regularly inviting family members around. You might be able to communicate worries and

manage money problems before they become out of control. Consider a potluck if you want to keep expenses down.

Watch the Grandchildren.
Consider providing child care if your adult children have jobs and young children of their own. You have the opportunity to get to know your grandchildren better by offering to watch their children while saving your adult children money.

Never forget that prior to providing resources to others, it is crucial to ensure the stability of your own finances. You might discover that some of the best methods to contribute don't require money.

Supporting someone you care about is a lovely thing to do, but it can also occasionally be difficult and frustrating. You might be concerned for their welfare, annoyed by their predicament, or guilty for not being able to do more. Keep in mind that you need to look after yourself as well and that you are not in charge of their happiness or recovery.

Providing practical assistance to a loved one that doesn't cost a lot of money or time is one approach to support them without endangering your retirement. For instance, you might offer to cook for them, do errands for them, or assist them with household duties. Without putting a strain on your resources or schedule, these actions can demonstrate your concern for them and lighten their load.

Making a secure space for your loved one to communicate their feelings and views without worrying about criticism or judgment is another approach to help them. To accomplish this, attentively listen to what they are saying, acknowledge their feelings, and refrain from offering unwelcome suggestions or downplaying their issues. Additionally, you can be genuine and upbeat with them and, if appropriate, share your own struggles and experiences. They may feel less alone and more hopeful as a result of this.

The last way you can help your loved one is by urging them to get professional assistance if they do. You can aid them in locating a therapist, support group, or community service that can offer them the necessary support and direction. Additionally, you may offer to go with them to their appointments or follow up with them frequently to see how they are doing. This can demonstrate to them your regard for their decisions and desire for their improvement.

It can be gratifying and pleasant to support someone you care about, but it can also be detrimental to your own physical and mental health. Setting appropriate limits with your loved one and engaging in self-care are so crucial. Making time for yourself, engaging in activities that bring you joy, and asking for assistance from others when necessary will help you do this. It's important to keep in mind that you can't give from an empty cup and that taking care of oneself is not selfish but vital.

In order to make your children's lives simpler, as a parent, you'd do almost everything, from helping them with their homework and taking them to soccer games when they were little to consoling their broken hearts or watching their kids when they became older.

However, a rising number of parents are choosing to support their adult children financially, even if doing so puts their own financial security in jeopardy.
For both parents and kids, these sacrifices can be risky.
According to financial experts, making such sacrifices can be harmful for both parents and

children. It's possible that the parents will end up burdening their children even more financially if they run out of money in retirement. And giving kids this kind of help can make it harder for them to become financially independent.

Helping your children is crucial, but if you mess it up, you might only have so many years to be able to make up for financial losses or correct the situation. With the exception of retirement, you may borrow money for almost everything in this world.

However, many parents still place a high importance on helping their adult children financially. Here's how to conduct yourself responsibly:

Financial Advantages and Disadvantages of Living with Parents

Recognize the Amount of Support You Can Afford.

Before giving your children money, run the figures yourself or with the help of a financial expert to understand the long-term financial impact.

In Jackson, Mississippi, at Anchor Pointe Wealth Management, certified financial planner J. Derieck Hodges says, "You don't want the parents to run out of money for themselves, or to run into a conflict with completing their own financial goals."

Even if the worst-case scenario doesn't occur, "Mom and Dad's lifestyle could be enough affected that they have to quit traveling or doing other things that they want to do in retirement," the author continues.

Once you realize that, you can make a decision that will depend on whether your child needs help with a one-time issue, like unforeseen medical expenses, or a persistent problem, like unmanageable credit card debt.
What to Do If You Have a Lot of Debt
Set goals and adhere to them.
It's crucial to let your children know how much you can provide and how long your support will last, especially for continuing financial agreements like helping with rent or a car payment. You can even think about progressively cutting back on how much you offer your kids.
I believes that helping others shouldn't be seen as a free pass or an endless source of revenue. "You need to establish precise boundaries."

Your kids will be more likely to concentrate on modifying their spending and way of life to survive without your financial support if they realize there is a limit to it.

Teach While Giving

There are methods to aid your children financially while simultaneously teaching them valuable lessons that will enable them to achieve financial independence.

For instance, if your child qualifies for a Roth IRA, you might volunteer to make contributions (up to $6,500 in 2023) on their behalf. This would allow them to free up some money in their budget and would also teach them the value of saving money for the future.

How to Teach Children About Money.

Be open and honest with your children about the effects on your finances.

Make sure they realize how providing that aid would impact your own financial security if your children ask for a sizable financial favor, such a down payment on a house or money for their children's tuition.

This will not only let you say "no" more readily if you can't provide them the level of assistance they request, but it will also impart to them an essential lesson about considering the long-term effects of their own financial commitments.

As Effectively as You Can Give.

You must submit a gift tax return to the IRS if you give an individual more than $17,000 (or $34,000 from both you and your spouse). However, there are several circumstances in which you are permitted to provide more than the allotted amount, such paying tuition directly to a school on someone else's behalf or paying medical bills directly to a healthcare provider. The lifetime exemption for gifts, however, is $12.92 million as of 2023.

Consider the financial ramifications of the transaction if selling investments is necessary to raise money for your children. For instance, you might not want to lock in the losses on investments whose value has decreased, but you also want to make sure that you have the money to pay the capital gains tax on investments whose value has improved over time.

According to a senior managing director in New York City, "there are a lot of potential land mines to consider when you're giving that type of donation." To avoid contributing more than you intended due to the cost to you, you must ensure that you are properly educated.

Way to support your adult kid

When I provide parenting coaching, I frequently hear from parents who are quite frustrated with their adult children for being blocked, silenced, and lacking any foreseen, practical strategies to become independent. In this article, I'll discuss ways to aid adult children who are having a hard time by dealing with their frequent denial, rage, and helplessness due to their lack of motivation. As independent adults with their own interests and wants, motivating an adult kid might be difficult. You can still encourage them by doing a few things, though.

Verify Your Communication.

Be receptive to your adult child's ideas and listen to their worries. Show them that you value their thoughts and that you can be a sounding board for answers. One customer, Lisa, learned how crucial it was to refrain from giving her 27-year-old daughter Annie career advice. Lisa was understandably concerned when Annie opted to discontinue her dental hygienist training. Annie revealed her desire to work with animals in the veterinary industry when Lisa changed from being an overbearing parent to a helpful emotion coach. Lisa then started to listen with validation.

Acknowledge when you are not being supportive.

Look in the accountability mirror to identify any times you fail to recognize or support your adult child's efforts and successes, no matter how minor. Serena believed she had always been behind her 26-year-old son Dante, who had dropped out of two colleges and a certificate program that was even shorter in order to pursue a career as a software engineer. When he explained his new decision to enlist in the military, Dante said to Serena that her tone seemed judgmental. After realizing her critical tone, Serena adjusted it. Dante investigated and determined that the military system was a suitable fit for him, and he moved on to develop high-tech talents through this path.

Give Perseverance Praise.
Grit is the tenacity and ardor for long-term objectives. It is the capacity to persist in a course of action in the face of hardship. Through effort, practice, and introspection, grit can be strengthened. Helping your adult child recognize the challenges they overcame in the past can give them the confidence to reflect and the tenacity to move forward. This was the situation with Edwin, a 33-year-old man who became sober and saw a work coach in order to "start my life over for the better.

Foster Independence.

Give your child the room and freedom to decide for themselves, and let them make errors in order to learn from them. Maintaining a good relationship with your child and being there for them when they need you are ultimately the most crucial factors. Instead of jumping in with solutions, let them work through their issues and provide guidance. Show confidence in their judgment and skills. Be open to dialogue and pay close attention to what they have to say.

Chapter 3

Maximizing your Employment Years

A key component of succeeding in the workplace is maximizing performance at work. There are actions you can do to improve your performance and raise your chances of success, whether you're a high-level executive or an entry-level employee. We'll go over some useful advice in this article that will help you perform at your best at work.

Land A Job As An Intern

Getting an internship with a big business in your field might be a fantastic opportunity. You can broaden your professional network while gaining knowledge about the techniques, procedures, and practices used in the sector. Adding important experience to your CV will help you stand out as a candidate when it comes time to start looking for a job. Try searching for internships in your area through local universities, job programs, or labor unions.

Develop Your Fundamental Competencies.

Think about your fundamental competencies as well as the soft and hard abilities you need to succeed in your position. Classes, mentors, and/or internships can help you develop and improve those talents. You might work on developing new fundamental skills during your free time to improve your employability. A young lawyer might read legal books, for instance, to better comprehend the rationale behind the operation of certain laws.

Expansion Of Professional Network

Increasing your professional network can assist you in making important connections in your field. Think about concentrating on going to business- and/or industry-related events, like seminars, workshops, and social gatherings. Use email lists or professional networking sites to try to connect with people online.

Advance In Your Organization

Moving to a position that you believe better suits your skills can be one way to advance in your organization, but it's not always a leadership position. You might choose to switch to a position that gives for greater creative flexibility or a parallel role within the business in a different department. Consider when and why you wish to advance, as well as the knowledge or actions required to get there.

Earn More Credentials

Having greater credentials in your sector can lead to new work and wage opportunities, making it one of the most popular instances of a professional objective. You may seek a master's degree to work as a professor at the nearby institution, for instance, if you already hold a bachelor's in civil engineering. Credibility in the sector can also be established with higher certifications.

Pay Yourself More Money.

A higher pay is something that many professionals strive for. You can increase your sense of security and self-assurance by working harder to earn more money. Think about your ideal wage, your current pay, and how you may work toward reaching it, whether in your current role or a new one.

Choose A Another Profession.

It's possible that your major professional objective should be to seek a completely other career path. A new career may bring you better happiness and satisfaction in addition to a higher compensation and more prospects. Think about how you can transition from your current employment to your desired profession. If you have contacts in other industries, think about reaching out to them to see if they might be a good fit for you.

Develop Your Subject-matter Expertise

Developing into an authority in your subject may open up a variety of job possibilities as well as additional options as a consultant or freelancer. To understand more about what industry professionals perform on a daily basis, investigate what qualifications or experience current industry experts hold and how you may achieve those credentials.

Take On A Position Of Leadership

Taking on a leadership role can help you develop your capacity for teamwork, collaboration, and leadership as well as build your reputation in the field. Take into account the kind of leadership role you desire and the path you might take to get there. It's critical to assess whether your employer provides these opportunities or if a career change may be necessary.

Take Home A Prize In Your Field

By increasing your employability, establishing your credentials as an industry expert, and gaining recognition from other industry professionals, winning an award can help you gain renown in the field. As an interior designer, for instance, winning an award might increase your visibility and open up more job options. Awards vary by industry, but winning one might include patience, competence, and invention in addition to other qualities.

Acquire A New Industry Skill.
Technologies that are developing frequently give industries new and creative tools. Learning one of these new skills can help you stand out from the competition for jobs and may even increase your compensation. Think about the most recent technological advancements in your field and look for ways to learn more about them or how to use them.

Launch A Business Using Your Abilities.
Starting a business is a key professional objective for some people. You can use your leadership abilities, along with other business-related skills, to launch your own company if you believe you have strong leadership qualities. Owning your own business can increase your level of creative control over your professional path, enable you to make more money, and offer you a more flexible work schedule.

Develop Your Teamwork Abilities
To develop cutting-edge products and services for the business, many positions rely on employee collaboration. When it comes to finishing tasks,

meeting deadlines, and developing new goods or services, collaboration skills can help you perform more effectively in a team environment. If there are any educational opportunities—such as seminars—that could improve your ability to collaborate, take them into account.

Create A Fresh Industry Benchmark

With new industry standards, many professionals hope to innovate their field. A factory worker might, for instance, try to innovate the manufacturing industry by developing a new, secure, and more cost-effective technique of quality assurance testing. Innovation can help you build your resume and improve your suitability as a candidate for future jobs. Try looking into innovative work practices that can boost output, worker security, or the caliber of goods and services.

Develop Your Personal Brand

Building your own brand can be different than launching a business. Some professionals build their reputation as authors, consultants, or subject matter experts in their fields, and they then use those abilities to look for new job openings and sources of revenue. Take into account how your personal brand might appear, how you can use it to progress your profession, and what abilities you will require to increase your credibility in the field.

Train As A Mentor

Some professionals use their knowledge and expertise to coach and advise the upcoming generation of industry leaders. Being a mentor can give you the opportunity to work closely with a newcomer to the sector and support them as they succeed in their role. By doing this, you can also widen your professional network and improve your own sense of career happiness.

Pursue Your Ideal Position

The ideal workplace, according to many experts, is their dream employment. Think about what your ideal career would be like, whether it be working for yourself or for a cutting-edge business in a certain sector. To start taking the steps to land your dream career, think about the qualifications the role could require and how you can meet them.

Minimize Idle Time And Interruptions

You can save time by minimizing interruptions and downtime at work, which might enable you to explore other opportunities and perform more efficiently. Social media is only one example of a personal distraction that you can identify and come up with solutions for. You could choose to completely eliminate the distraction or set time limits on specific diversions.

Form A New Work Routine

You may increase your productivity and establish better work habits to advance your career by changing your current routines. To enhance your daily word count and productivity, for instance, you may make it a habit to write an extra piece each day. This will allow you to pursue a higher position in your writing organization. Developing new habits can benefit your career development and boost your employability.

Establish Definite Objectives

The first step in maximizing your performance at work is to set goals that are precise and doable. This will make it easier for you to concentrate on your goals and make sure you are moving toward a particular result. It's crucial to make sure your goals are SMART (specific, measurable, achievable, relevant, and time-bound). SMART objectives provide you a clear direction and a schedule for your job. They give you the ability to monitor your development and adapt as necessary to stay on course.

Effectively Manage Your Time

For you to perform at your best at work, effective time management is a need. You may get more done in less time by learning how to prioritize your activities, cut out distractions, and manage your time well. Make a to-do list first, then prioritize items based on importance and urgency. To help you remain on track and fulfill deadlines, use tools like calendars, timers, and reminders.

Develop Effective Communication Skills

Success in the job depends on having effective communication. It promotes interpersonal harmony, helps to settle disputes, and keeps everyone on the same page. Concentrate on speaking clearly and simply, listening actively, and utilizing proper body language while you communicate. Accept criticism well and don't hesitate to seek for clarification when necessary.

Create Stable Relationships

The key to maximizing your effectiveness at work is developing excellent relationships with your coworkers, bosses, and clients. Strong relationships increase your chances of getting encouragement, criticism, and development opportunities. Be a good listener, exhibit empathy, and engage in proactive communication with others if you want to develop solid relationships.

Constantly Improve Your Knowledge and Skills

Continuous learning and skill development are crucial if you want to maintain your competitiveness in the fast-paced workplace of today. Keep up with the most recent developments in your profession by attending training sessions, reading books, and enrolling in online courses. To pinpoint areas for development and focus on acquiring new abilities to stay relevant, get feedback from your bosses and coworkers.

Work As A Team Player

For you to perform at your best at work, you must be a team player. It entails having the willingness to cooperate, impart ideas, and assist your coworkers. You are more likely to accomplish your goals and flourish as a team when you get along with other people. Building trusting connections with your coworkers, being receptive to criticism, and being willing to take on responsibilities outside of your job description are all important aspects of being a team player.

Look After Your Well-being And Health

To perform at your best at work, you must prioritize your health and well-being. You are more productive and concentrated when you are healthy and energized. To keep your body in good shape, be sure to get enough sleep, eat well, and exercise frequently. To refuel your batteries and lower your stress levels, take pauses throughout the day.

It takes a combination of abilities, routines, and actions to perform at your best at work. You can improve your chances of success at work by establishing clear goals, effectively managing your time, mastering good communication techniques, fostering strong interpersonal relationships, constantly learning and honing your skills, being a team player, and attending to your health and wellbeing. Recall that success is a process rather than a final goal. Achieving your goals and maximizing your performance at work requires time, effort, and commitment.

Chapter 4
Living Situation

Don't put off seeking care until you are in a position where you must act swiftly. Instead, spend some time right now to decide which of these senior home options is best for you.

Aging at home.

Relocating with the children.

Shared housing

Autonomous housing complexes.

Senior housing.

Life-plan neighborhoods.

Affordable housing

Aging at home

Many homes may be made secure and welcoming places for retirees to live with a few adjustments, such as moving a bedroom on the main floor and adding grab bars to the toilet.

Think about broad pathways, advises Hutter. "Consider how you enter and exit the house."

Some groups might provide home evaluations and offer suggestions on what renovations might be necessary to allow an elderly person to live in safety there for the foreseeable future. Additionally, occupational or vocational therapists might provide this service.

The practice of "**Aging In Place**" may involve more than simple house improvements; elderly Americans may eventually require in-home care. Workers in the personal care industry provide services like cooking, cleaning, and errand running. Some organizations may be able to offer therapists and nurses who can help with medication or other hands-on requirements to folks who require expert care.

The expense of home improvements and in-home care can strain a senior's already tight budget, but older homeowners may be able to borrow against the equity in their homes to offset the expenditures.Based on the equity in their house, reverse mortgages might offer seniors a flat sum, a line of credit, or monthly payments. The property is often sold to pay off the loan whenever the owner vacates the property or passes away.

Before obtaining a reverse mortgage, make sure you are aware of the fees and conditions. Seniors may find these loans to be a useful financial tool, but they may also be more expensive than other lending options.

Relocating With The Children

According to Susan Dolton, corporate director of sales at Goodwin Living, it's common for parents to think they can move in with an adult kid. Their older children might not agree, she adds.

However, living with an adult child or having them live with you might be beneficial for both parties. It can instantly cut living costs in half. Additionally, there's a chance that both parties will receive side advantages. While seniors, especially those who are single, benefit from an active household that will prevent loneliness and the health concerns associated with it, busy parents may find themselves with built-in childcare.

However, it's not always the case. Living with your adult children may result in frequent home alone times, according to Dolton. This can be the situation if your adult child travels frequently for business or if your health or mobility prevents you from accompanying the family on outings.
Setting up clear rules from the beginning is essential to make these arrangements work. Make sure everyone is on the same page with regard to

sharing expenses, personal space, and communal living.

Shared Housing

Consider renting a space with another senior if you'd prefer not to live with a family member. While moving in with the kids might have complex relationship dynamics, home sharing with another retiree offers comparable financial advantages.

Renters can half their monthly spending, while seniors who still own their homes may be able to locate a housemate to help with part of their living costs. Websites like Silvernest and Senior Homeshares are made exclusively for older people who wish to rent out space to people in the same demographic or are looking for roommates.

According to Johansen, "you need people who are all quite self-sufficient and at the same degree of care." One danger of living together is that if one person's health or capacity deteriorates, their housemate may end up taking care of them.

Communities of Independent Living

Senior apartments, retirement complexes, and active adult communities are just a few of the independent living options available to seniors. According to Johansen, "I like to think of senior housing as a continuum.

Senior apartments in age-restricted complexes are the first type in the category. These buildings might contain a pool or a gym, but they don't provide any other services like meals or transportation.

Then there are independent living neighborhoods, which go by many different names. Retirement communities, active adult neighborhoods, or senior housing are some names for them. Although residents have their own private living area, they also have access to community facilities including restaurants, golf courses, and theaters. The inhabitants may also have access to organized social events and outings.

Although huge suburban developments are sometimes linked with retirement communities, retirees do have the option to stay in cities if they so choose. It may be possible to renovate old schools, hospitals, and other downtown locations into new senior housing. While some construction projects cater to premium clients, others design homes that serve the medium market.

Many neighborhoods keep a busy calendar of events to encourage inhabitants to socialize and form connections. Because of this, anyone worried about social isolation should consider an independent living complex rather than a senior apartment building.

Senior Living

While independent living facilities provide a wealth of amenities, care services are often not offered there. Assisted living could be the ideal housing option for people who require assistance with daily duties.

Residents of these buildings may have private apartments as well as shared areas for dining and social gatherings. Housekeeping, personal hygiene, and medicine reminders are just a few of the chores that staff members can assist with. Facilities for assisted living are prepared to care for residents with a range of health issues, including cognitive impairment. According to Johansen, a tiny fraction of most assisted living communities today's communities is devoted to memory care.

Seniors have the option of living in a residential care facility in addition to standard assisted living facilities. There are many names for them, but they often have smaller settings and fewer individuals who might share rooms. In addition to providing what Johansen refers to as "at your elbow service" and continual supervision, it may be more cheap than a larger facility.

Between independent living and nursing facility care, assisted living care frequently acts as a transitional service. Some facilities may have an admission fee, and the monthly cost could include utilities and meals as well. A long-term care insurance policy might pay for assisted living even while Medicare won't.

Communities with a Life Plan
Life plan communities, sometimes referred to as continuing care retirement communities (CCRCs), bring together a variety of housing options on a single site to enable seniors to transition from independent living to assisted living to skilled nursing care, as needed. Some neighborhoods offer meals as well as other activities and are all-inclusive.

The founder and chairman emeritus of the financial planning firm Armstrong, Fleming & Moore in Washington, D.C., Alexandra Armstrong, claims that "CCRCs offer a tiered approach to the aging process, accommodating residents' demands as they age." "Each town has different coverage, so you should examine the specifics."

These communities might have contracts with various terms set up for them. While some impose an entrance fee and a subsequent monthly fee, others demand the purchase of a home within the community. Depending on the contract, that fee could increase as a resident's demands develop or it might remain the same regardless of the degree of care offered. Some communities have foundations or help programs to cover the expense if a resident reaches a point when they can no longer afford that fee.

Whether a community is for-profit or not-for-profit may determine whether it has a foundation. Dolton asserts that for-profit organizations may have shareholders, be owned by one organization, and be governed by a different one. Mission-driven not-for-profit communities are frequently but not necessarily faith-based. Prior to signing a contract, spend some time learning more about a community and what happens if a person runs out of money.

Housing on Subsidy

Several municipal, state, and federal housing programs may offer senior housing that is dependent on income. However, navigating subsidized housing programs may be challenging at all levels. Each may have a different set of requirements and an application process.

Don't wait to apply even if you believe it will be years before you require subsidized housing; waiting lists can be very extensive. For instance, Hutter points out that there aren't many reputable facilities taking part in the federal government's Section 8 housing program, and those that do may have long waiting lists.

Chapter 5

How to maintain financial security in retirement

Nearly all of the recent study on the subject indicates that most people lack the ability to show they are financially secure, especially during their retirement years. This just serves to highlight the fact that gaining financial security is a difficult process that demands careful preparation and execution.

Without a doubt, what various people mean by "financial security" varies. However, we'll stick to a straightforward definition: having sufficient financial resources to pay your costs, unanticipated bills, and retirement without having to worry about running out.

POINTS TO NOTE

It goes without saying that starting to save early is best, but you can start saving at any age.

Try thinking of your retirement savings as a regular expense, much like paying rent, a mortgage, or a car loan, to make saving easier.

It's a good idea to reevaluate your financial profile and, if necessary, make adjustments if your lifestyle, income, or financial responsibilities have changed.

Consider increasing the amount you save in tax-deferred accounts if you have enough income.

The appropriate asset mix takes into account your age, risk tolerance, and whether you need your assets to increase in value or provide income.

If you are married, think about whether your partner is also putting money away and whether some expenses can be split throughout your retirement years.

It will be important to hire the services of an experienced and qualified financial planner if you lack experience in the area of financial planning and portfolio management.

1. Begin as soon as you can.

Although it goes without saying that beginning to save early is preferable, it is never too late to start—even if you are already close to retirement—because every dollar saved helps to pay your costs.

You will have saved a lot more money if you save $200 per month for 40 years at 5% interest than if you save the same amount for only 10 years. The money saved over a shorter period, however, can make a significant contribution to helping to pay for costs in retirement.

As you approach closer to retirement, keep in mind that other aspects of financial planning, such asset allocation, will become more crucial. This is because as the number of years you have to make up any losses diminishes, your risk tolerance usually increases.

2. Treat savings accounts like bills.

Regularly saving money can be difficult when there are so many bills that we all have to pay for on a regular basis, not to mention all the tempting consumer products that tempt us to spend our money.

By approaching your retirement savings as a monthly obligation, much like paying rent, a mortgage, or a car loan, you may avoid giving in to this temptation. This is even simpler if your employer automatically deducts the sum from your paycheck.

The amount of income taxes due on your salary are decreased if the deduction is made pre-tax from your paycheck.

You can also choose to have your paycheck deposited directly into a bank or savings account as an alternative (or in addition). Additionally, you can arrange for the desired savings amount to be automatically debited from the retirement savings account on the same day that the pay is credited.

3. Contribute to a tax-deferred account.

By making contributions to a tax-deferred retirement account using money set aside for retirement, you can avoid paying taxes and penalties on impulsive purchases.

For instance, any money withdrawn from a typical retirement account may be taxed in the year it is received, and if you are younger than age 5912 at the time of the distribution, a 10% early distribution penalty (excise tax) may apply.

Consider increasing the amount you save in tax-deferred accounts if you have enough income. Consider if you can afford to contribute to an individual retirement account (IRA) in addition to saving money in an employer-sponsored retirement plan, and whether a Roth IRA or a regular IRA should be used for the IRA.

4. Expand Your Portfolio's Range

Retirement assets are a good example of when the proverb "don't put all of your eggs in one basket" applies. Investing all of your savings in one thing raises your chance of losing everything and could reduce your return on investment (ROI).As a result, managing your retirement funds includes asset allocation as a vital component. Proper asset allocation takes into account the following elements:

Your age: This is typically mirrored in your portfolio's level of aggressiveness, which will probably take more risks when you're younger and less as you approach closer to retirement age.

Your level of risk tolerance: This makes sure that if losses do occur, they do so when there is still time to recover from them.

Whether you require revenue generation or wealth growth.

5. Take into account all feasible expenses

Some of us make the error of forgetting to budget for income taxes, long-term care, and health and dental expenses while planning for retirement.

Make a note of all the expenses you might have throughout your retirement years before estimating how much you need to save. You can then prepare appropriately and generate realistic estimates as a result.

6. Retirement savings are essential

Saving a lot of money is fantastic, but the advantages are diminished or even eliminated if you have to take out high-interest loans to cover your living needs.

So it's crucial to plan ahead and stick to a budget. To ensure that your projected recurring expenses are properly taken into account when determining your disposable income, your retirement savings should be included.

7. Routinely Review Your Portfolio

Strategic asset allocation must be done on your portfolio to allow for any necessary adjustments as you approach closer to retirement and your financial demands, costs, and risk tolerance change. This will assist you in making sure your retirement planning is on track.

8. Cut Your Costs Where You Can

Reevaluating your financial profile and making any necessary adjustments to change the amounts you contribute to your retirement nest egg may be a good idea if your lifestyle, income, or financial responsibilities have changed. For instance, you might have paid off your vehicle loan or mortgage, or the number of people for whom you are financially responsible might have changed.

To establish if you need to increase or decrease the amount you save on a regular basis, you should reevaluate your income, expenses, and financial commitments.

9. Keep Your Spouse in Mind

If you are married, think about whether your partner is also putting money away and whether some expenses can be split throughout your retirement years. If your spouse hasn't been saving, you need to figure out if your retirement funds can pay for both your and your spouse's costs.

10. Consult a financial planner

It will be important to hire the services of an experienced and qualified financial planner if you lack experience in the area of financial planning and portfolio management. One of the most crucial choices you'll have to make is which partner is suitable for you.

11. Understand your costs
You are now aware of your monthly spending. You must estimate your monthly expenses when you leave your employment in order to properly plan for retirement. Can you cut any expenses from your budget, such as a monthly parking pass? Are there any expenses, such as your wardrobe budget, that are expected to go down?

Start by sitting down and listing all the expenses you'll have in retirement. This covers your remaining costs for housing, electricity, food,

Medicare premiums, medical care, taxes, and any other expenses. Don't forget to budget extra for activities like travel, friend lunches, golf, or anything else you have on your bucket list.

12. Determine your reliable sources of revenue.
Where will you get your retirement income? You might have Social Security payments, a pension, annuities, rental income, a retirement account, or another reliable source of income, for instance.

13. Use your assured income to cover your set living expenses.
Fixed, variable, and one-time expenses are the three different categories. Monthly recurring costs are known as fixed expenses. Orman advises ensuring you have enough assured income to cover your set expenses once you've determined what they will be.

Money that is guaranteed to be paid to you each month for the rest of your life. Social Security, pensions, and annuities are a few examples.

The wisdom of Orman's counsel is as follows: You won't have to worry about taking money out of your retirement account to pay your bills if you can afford to cover your monthly obligations with assured income. Your retirement savings will still be available to you, but you can use those assets anyway you see fit.

14. Maintain two years' worth of cash reserves.
Your retirement, Orman says. Not your portfolio. She is implying that using assured income to pay your bills entails letting any retirement savings continue to grow. That aim to allow retirement assets to develop is the basis for her suggestion to keep two years' worth of living costs in cash.

Consider that your retirement savings lose value if another epidemic strikes or if the United States experiences a recession the year after you retire. The absolute worst time to withdraw funds from your investments is then. If you're able to keep your retirement funds in place, you can utilize them to buy stocks and other assets for dirt cheap. When the stock market recovers, your portfolio will be even more valuable.

Keeping two years' worth of living expenses in cash allows you to access those money without having to deplete your retirement savings.

15. Create an RMD strategy

Required Minimum Distributions is what they call it. Once they turn 72, a retiree must take out at least this much each year from their tax-advantaged retirement plan. (According to Fidelity, a tax-advantaged retirement account enables tax-free growth or tax-deferred savings.)

When you become 72, you'll have to start taking withdrawals. There are three different withdrawal options: lump amount, monthly, and quarterly. Making the withdrawals prior to the annual deadline is a crucial reminder. Uncle Sam imposes some severe consequences for failure to comply.

One of the various online RMD calculators, like this one provided by AARP, is the simplest way to determine your RMD for the year.

There is no cap on the amount you can withdraw, however failing to withdraw the minimum will result in a severe penalty.

16. Set a limit of 4% of your wealth as spending during the first year of retirement.
Now that you've officially retired, you're eager to do everything you were unable to do while you were working. However, such goods will be expensive. Orman advises against using your first year of

retirement as a means of living your dreams. Plan to take no more than 4%, instead. For instance, you won't take more than $25,500 if your portfolio is worth $800,000.

Keep in mind that you will owe taxes on any money you withdraw from an account that was funded with pre-tax dollars.

Building a house brick by brick is similar to preparing for retirement. It may take years to complete, but the more effort you put into it, the safer you will be.

Chapter 6
The 50-year-old Power Moves

It's simple to convince yourself that there's no need to start saving for retirement while you're young. But before you realize it, you can be in your 50s and still far from your retirement savings target.
Even early savers might worry about not having enough money saved for their golden years. According to a NerdWallet survey, only 20% of respondents aged 45 to 54 indicated they were certain they had enough saved for retirement in the previous year.

You may increase your nest egg if you're in your fifties and feel like you're falling behind on your savings. Use an online calculator, like FINRA's Retirement Calculator, to determine how much you should be saving based on your present age, income, and desired retirement age.

Here are five ideas to help you catch up if you think you might fall short:

1. Increase your contributions to tax-advantaged retirement accounts.

Increased contributions to tax-advantaged plans, such as IRAs and 401(k)s offered via employers, are a terrific method to catch up. You may contribute more than the maximum annual contribution limit if you are 50 years of age or older.For IRS contribution limits, visit this page.

It can be challenging to put aside that extra money, but it's crucial to keep in mind that if you put $7,000 into a traditional 401(k) or another tax-advantaged account, the tax savings will reduce your annual income by less than $7,000 (exact amounts depend on your tax bracket and financial situation). To determine whether you're on pace to save as much as is permitted, utilize the FINRA "401(k) Save the Max" calculator.

2. Look for ways to reduce expenses

By reducing your current spending, you can increase your retirement savings as well. Start by carefully examining your present spending plan.What is coming in and what is going out affects the budget. You can, with discipline, transfer that money into a retirement savings account in its place if you can reduce part of your spending (what goes out).

Fortunately, some expenses, such as the cost of driving to work, might go down once you retire. If these adjustments aren't significant enough to have an impact on your retirement funds, you might need to think about making further significant reductions once you retire.

For instance, you can think about buying a less expensive home, giving up your automobile, or relocating to a more walkable neighborhood.

3. Take into account working more or longer.

The ability to save more money and more time for retirement is one of the clear benefits of working longer hours. Another advantage is that the longer you wait to start getting Social Security payments after reaching full retirement age, the more money you'll get when you do. This increase is two-thirds of one percent for every month you put off getting benefits, or eight percent every year, until you turn 70.

Consider adding more gig economy "jobs" now or during retirement if you decide against working longer in your current position. Examples include driving for a ride sharing firm or doing other freelance work. This will help you delay the time when you begin getting Social Security payments.

4. Be serious about your "extra" cash

Avoid the temptation to overspend if you get a raise, an inheritance, a bonus, or a tax return. Instead, put that extra money toward your retirement, ideally into an account that offers tax benefits. Never pass up an opportunity to make your money work for you in order to have a stable financial future.

5. Assess Investment Fees

It costs money to invest. There are numerous costs that could be associated with various account types, and these investing fees might have a surprisingly significant impact on your returns. To make sure that hefty fees aren't steadily eating away at your money, it's a good idea to periodically check your financial accounts.

By allowing you to compare more than 20,000 mutual funds and exchange-traded products, FINRA's Fund Analyzer can help you understand fees. When it comes to investments you make on your own, you definitely have control over costs, although you may not have much of that influence in an employer-sponsored retirement plan.

Think about a 50-year-old who starts off with $300,000 in retirement savings and contributes $25,000 a year. Over the next 15 years, nearly $130,000 of the portfolio's value will be lost to fees if the account generates an average yearly return of 7 percent and pays 1 percent in fees. In contrast, if the hypothetical 50-year-old had the same retirement account but paid a cost of 0.6 percent, over the course of 15 years, just around $66,000 would go to fees, leaving her with an additional $60,000 in retirement savings.

Chapter 7

The best places to invest

Since people are living longer, your retirement savings may need to last for 20 years or longer.

Bonds, annuities, and income-producing stocks can provide retirement income in addition to Social Security, a pension, savings, and other investments for people who are approaching or have reached retirement.

You can choose the best retirement income strategy with the assistance of a financial expert.

In the US, a person who turns 65 may expect to live for about 85 years on average. The average is just that.

Today, one in three 65-year-olds will live to be at least 90 years old, and one in seven will live to be at least 95. Many people who want to retire in their 60s still need to make their retirement savings endure over 30 years. That puts a lot of strain on a conventional retirement plan.

Only around 40% of your pre-retirement earnings will be replaced by Social Security retirement payments. With a pension, savings, or investments, you'll need to augment your benefits.

Only around 40% of your pre-retirement wages will be replaced by Social Security retirement benefits; for a retiree making $100,000 per year, Social Security will only replace 33% of pre-retirement earnings. These benefits tend to be more significant for lower wage earners. With a pension (if available), savings, or investments, you'll need to augment your benefits.

For a variety of factors, including the advantages to their health and finances of participating in their communities and remaining active. Nevertheless, it's crucial to have a strategy in place for producing extra income during retirement and making sure that future revenue streams can keep up with escalating living expenditures.

According to Rob Haworth, senior investment strategy director at U.S. Bank, "people are understanding that they may generate more competitive income while reducing volatility in their portfolio in today's interest rate environment." Investors developing a strategy for retirement income should reevaluate their options in light of the large increase in interest rates.

Here are four popular investing strategies for you to consider in order to supplement your retirement income, generally arranged from lower to higher risk.

Income annuities

In exchange for regular income distributions, you and an insurance company enter into a contract in which you pay a lump sum, either all at once or monthly. You can use annuities to create a guaranteed income stream for the rest of your life or for a specific amount of time. You can also decide whether this income will be paid throughout the course of your lifetime alone or the lifetimes of both you and another person (such as your spouse).

Depending on the type of annuity, you pay a certain sum to an insurance company with the idea that you will receive the money either right away or at a later time. The funds may grow tax-deferred while they are in the insurance company's possession. You can select a fixed dollar amount on a regular basis or one that is adjusted for inflation when you begin taking disbursements. You can get assistance from a financial expert in deciding which kind of annuity best suits your requirements.

For certain of your retirement assets, annuities might offer security, long-term growth, and income. Annuities are frequently used by retirees as a supplement to other guaranteed income sources (like Social Security) to help pay for non-discretionary expenses. Since they guarantee your income, they are sometimes viewed as a type of insurance against the possibility that you would outlive your retirement resources.

A reliable, regular source of income in retirement, irrespective of market changes, is something annuities may offer.

taxable income as well as tax-deferred growth.

flexibility in how you pay for retirement and save for it.

the likelihood that payments to beneficiaries will go on after your death.

Annuities' problems:

The underlying insurance company's capacity to pay claims is a condition of any guarantees.

There could be little liquidity.

A 10% tax penalty may apply to annuity withdrawals made before the age of 59 1/2.

If your annuity isn't underwritten by a reputable insurance provider, the risks could be higher.

2. An array of different bond holdings

Bonds and other fixed income investments were formerly thought to be less competitive as a retirement income source. But the Federal Reserve increased the short-term interest rate. For instance, the yield on a 5-year U.S. Treasury note was 1.37% at the start of 2022 and increased to 3.74% by the end of May 2023.

Bonds come in a variety of formats. You can directly invest in individual bonds such as U.S. Treasury securities, municipal bonds, debt obligations issued by corporations, government-offered bonds, mortgage-backed securities, and bonds with origins in foreign markets. The bond's tenure (number of years to maturity) and market circumstances, as well as the issuer's creditworthiness, all influence yields. Many investors opt to place their money in bond mutual funds, which are professionally managed portfolios of bonds from several issuers.

The bond issuer will send you periodic income payments depending on the stated annual yield in effect at the time of your investment. The issuing entity will repay the principal if you decide to hold the bond until it matures. As an alternative, you could decide to sell bonds on the open market before they mature.

Depending on the interest rate environment and the length of the bond's remaining term, a bond's market value may differ from its face value. An existing bond will have to sell at a discount in order to draw buyers if current market rates are higher than the yield on the bond. The bond will sell for more money if current interest rates are higher than its yield. This highlights a crucial fact that bond investors frequently miss: while being viewed as a lower-risk investment, bonds can experience price fluctuations.

A consistent income stream with potentially attractive yields are two things bonds can offer.
flexibility in liquidity to adjust the composition of a portfolio at the right time.
the ability to choose from a variety of fixed income securities with various risk and yield profiles.
the capacity to effectively diversify a portfolio of securities, including securities from different asset classes and stocks, to help reduce risk.
Bonding difficulties:
Income paid to you is taxable at standard income tax rates, with the exception of municipal bonds that are tax-free.

if interest rates rise and the investor needs to sell the bond, there is a chance of losing principal.
challenges in replacing maturing bonds with income that is comparable in the future.
Lack of protection from inflation because stable revenue streams from a bond portfolio.

3. Total return on investment
Interest, dividends, and capital gains are all ways that a total return strategy might generate income from your investment portfolio. This kind of portfolio makes investments in stock and bond funds that are both diverse and in a balanced ratio.

In this context, the term "total return" refers to the expenditure of a portion of the average yearly rate of returns (income and appreciation) over a longer time frame (10–20 years), as opposed to focusing on particular annual return rates or only taking income from portfolio holdings. The objective is for this total return to equal or surpass your withdrawal rate.

As Haworth explains, "this is a technique to expand a retirement portfolio to ensure that it continues to satisfy the demands of persons preparing for a retirement that could last for 20 to 30 years or longer." In comparison to other investment strategies typically used in retirement, it might provide a technique to produce a greater overall return.

A total return model, which closely resembles a, follows a, where a portion of your investment is distributed annually. The payout amount typically falls between 3 and 5% of the portfolio's overall value.

A total return strategy can offer you: A solution to meet your short-term cash flow requirements while continuing to save money for expenses that will probably increase over time due to inflation.
the potential to use a wider variety of assets than is possible with more traditional methods to retirement income.
a steady stream of portfolio withdrawals that can be more tax-efficient because they are likely to be driven mostly by capital growth.
the difficulties of a total return strategy
The longevity of your savings throughout retirement is not guaranteed.
There is no set rate of withdrawal, thus the amount of your return may change from year to year.
Assets may exhaust before retirement is over, especially if assets perform poorly.

4. Equities that generate income

While the main reason people invest in stocks is to increase the value of their portfolio, some stocks also offer dividend payments. Paying dividends to shareholders is a common practice for publicly traded firms to distribute their profits. Stocks that do pay dividends tend to do so in different ways and at different rates depending on the stock.

When the bond market endured an unusually low interest rate environment, Haworth claims that stock dividends "become substantially more enticing." Although most stock dividend yields today are not as competitive as bond yields, they nevertheless have the potential to increase in value.

Quarterly dividend payments are the norm for businesses. Although it happens seldom and you shouldn't bank on it, firms occasionally pay a "special dividend" because of exceptional circumstances. But unlike most bonds, stock dividends can change with each payout period, and corporations do occasionally stop paying dividends. With regard to dividend payouts, you must be ready for some degree of uncertainty.

Examining a stock's dividend payment history is crucial if your primary goal is to invest in it for income. The most appealing stocks to consider for this purpose are probably those that have a track record of consistently paying out dividends or continuously growing dividend payouts.

The sort of income-producing equity known as publicly listed real estate investment trusts, or, can further diversify a portfolio made up mostly of equities and bonds. A company called a REIT owns, manages, or finances real estate that generates revenue.

Publicly-traded REITs are listed on significant stock exchanges, making it simple to buy and sell them just like stocks. Daily changes in price are common. According to Haworth, "This price fluctuation is a worry for investors, as it is not merely the underlying value of the assets housed in the REIT that impacts the price." "External variables that affect the overall investment climate may have an impact on the price you pay for a REIT or the price you receive when you sell one," according to the statement.

Equities that generate income can give you:

a dependable source of income provided by corporations that produce significant profits and consistently pay dividends.

having the chance to profit from the prospective capital growth of income-producing equities.

a "built-in return" on your equity investment that is represented by dividend income and independent of the success of the stock price.

Publicly traded REITs offer diversification for a portfolio that is mostly made up of stocks and bonds; they are a diverse source of income for retirement portfolios.

Income-producing stock market difficulties:

Principal value is more susceptible to change than other conventional income sources like bonds.

Not all businesses consistently and dependable give out dividends.

As interest rates rise, stock dividends can start to seem less appealing.

Ordinary income tax rates on dividends are higher than those on other income.

Chapter 8

How to choose a Financial Advisor: The best financial advisor to work with.

The excellent, the bad, and the uncontrolled financial advisors
According to U.S. Securities and Exchange Commission regulations, any financial expert or company that engages in the business of giving advice to others or publishing securities reports or analyses for compensation is technically a "investment adviser" and is required to register with the SEC or their state, depending on the amount of assets the advisor manages, either through the SEC or their state.

Other titles and types of advise, however, are mostly unregulated, thus it is the investor's job to be aware of what to look for. Here are some recommendations:

1. Titles might not be important.

The phrase "financial advisor" itself and some of the most popular titles advisors employ aren't connected to any particular qualifications. Don't assume that someone who uses a title that seems official has received special instruction, a license, or registration.

2. Recognize the type of advice you require.

Finding the proper fit for you might be a lot easier if you know what you want from an advisor. For instance, if you need assistance with your taxes, you should look for a financial advisor that specializes in this area and possesses the necessary credentials. The best option may be a low-cost service like a robo-advisor if all you need is investment management. (Find out more information about how to pick a financial advisor.)

3. Track down a fee-only fiduciary.

Some financial advisors have an obligation to act in their clients' best interests rather than their own, known as a fiduciary duty. We advise working with a professional, registered fiduciary at all times; ideally one that is fee-only, meaning that you pay the advisor directly and not through commissions for certain investment or insurance products.

4. Research the adviser.

No matter what title, classification, certification, or license an advisor professes to hold, it is your responsibility to investigate the advisor's background and qualifications. Before agreeing to work with an advisor, always do your homework on them. Below are some resources for accomplishing it.

Several kinds of financial counselors

The most popular categories of financial advisors and what they perform are listed below.

1. Investment consultants

The SEC uses the phrase "investment adviser" legally to refer to a financial expert who needs to be registered, but it is also regularly used as a job title and is more typically spelled "advisor." A person or business that receives compensation for advising clients on investments is known as an investment advisor. Investment advisers have the ability to directly handle client money. The Financial Industry Regulatory Authority's BrokerCheck service allows you to confirm an advisor's registration, and you should do so.

2. Brokers and dealer-brokers

An individual or business that buys and sells assets including stocks, bonds, and mutual funds is known as a broker-dealer. Broker-dealers have the option of acting as a dealer, a broker, or both when buying and selling on behalf of clients. In addition to being SEC-registered, broker-dealers frequently belong to FINRA.

Depending on their licensing, broker-dealer representatives may only sell certain financial products. For instance, a broker-dealer who has passed the Series 6 exam can only market mutual funds, variable annuities, and associated goods. The holder of a Series 7 license may sell more securities. Another tool for broker verification is BrokerCheck.

3. a licensed financial advisor

CFPs hold themselves to a high standard of ethics and have completed the demanding training and experience criteria set forth by the CFP Board. To their clients, CFPs owe a fiduciary duty.

Financial planners can provide non-regulated services including advice on how to manage debt, prepare for retirement, or make a budget, but some of them also act as investment advisors. Be aware that financial advisors who do not hold the CFP designation may still use the term "financial planner" in their title. Make sure to verify a CFP's credentials with the CFP Board if you're especially seeking for one.

When possible, NerdWallet advises consulting with a CFP if you need a financial advisor.

4. Financial advisor

Anybody may use the general phrase "financial consultant." However, some financial advisors possess the title of chartered financial consultant, or ChFC. The educational requirements for chartered financial consultants are comparable to those for CFPs. ChFCs have a fiduciary duty and are required to follow the moral standards of The American College. Here, you can check the credentials of a ChFC.

5. Financial advisor

The most approachable financial professionals are frequently financial coaches. Financial literacy basics like how to save money or cut back on spending are the main focus of financial trainers.

Financial coaches can assist their clients in accumulating wealth, which they may later manage with the assistance of an investment advisor.

6. Asset, investment, and portfolio managers

Whether the title on the business card is asset manager, investment manager, or portfolio manager, these individuals handle the financial portfolios of their clients. In addition to managing a client's investment portfolio, a portfolio manager or investment manager may also provide additional financial planning services.

Investment and portfolio managers are likely to provide investment advice and would therefore be registered as investment advisors; nevertheless, you should always confirm this with BrokerCheck.

7. Financial advisors

Wealth managers and wealth advisers often work with highly rich customers and provide both investment advice and comprehensive financial planning services. When it comes to their clients' finances, wealth managers and advisers frequently offer services including estate planning, tax preparation, charitable giving, and even health insurance. The majority of wealth managers require a minimum investment of millions.

8. Robot adviser

A low-cost automated investment management service is a robo-advisor. For as little as 0.25% of your account balance each year, robo-advisors build and manage an investing portfolio based on your goals using computer algorithms. A robo-advisor might be the best choice for you if all you need help with is investment management.

9. A financial counselor

To help you develop a better money perspective, a financial therapist combines behavioral therapy and financial coaching. Financial therapists are aware that saving, investing, and setting a budget can bring up challenging sentiments, and they can support you while you work through trauma and other unpleasant emotions related to money.

List of Best Advisor Firm
Financial planners may help you with a variety of financial matters, including retirement planning, education savings for children, and investing in general. Finding a financial advisor to work with can

be difficult, though, as there are hundreds of thousands of them to pick from around the United States. The caliber of a financial advisor might fluctuate significantly from one firm to the next and even amongst advisors at the same organization. For your different financial needs, Bankrate has reviewed dozens of financial advisory firms and selected some of the top ones.

Below are the top advisors for 2023.
Vanguard
Vanguard may be most known for the wide range of inexpensive fund options it provides, but it also provides a number of various financial advisor solutions to suit the needs of a range of consumers. With minimum asset levels ranging from $50,000 to $5 million, Vanguard offers three different tiers of service that let you speak with a financial advisor. All three service tiers give customers access to customized financial planning, a range of investment choices, and automated tax loss harvesting.

The Personal Advisor Select program from Vanguard, which has a $500,000 investment requirement, is the only option if you're searching for a committed advisor to work with over time. Vanguard's Personal Advisor Wealth Management services are required by those seeking more complex financial guidance, such as guidance on estate planning or charitable giving. As your assets increase, the annual costs for all of Vanguard's financial adviser alternatives decrease and range from 0.30 percent to 0.40 percent.

AUM: $118.9 billion in clients' discretionary assets
Minimum balances range from $50,000 to $5 million depending on the level of assistance.
Charges: 0.30 to 0.40 percent
Schwab, Charles
You can locate financial adviser options that suit your demands in addition to Charles Schwab's platform, which is among the best for online brokerage. You can create a financial plan and sort through various investment possibilities with the assistance of a Schwab financial counselor, who is free to use for clients with $500,000 in assets. The yearly price for Schwab Wealth Advisory, which offers an even more individualized approach, is 0.80 and starts at $1 million in assets; the rate decreases as asset levels increase.

By using the website findyourindependentadvisor.com, Schwab can assist you in finding a local independent financial advisor. However, these advisors' fees could be considerably greater than those for Schwab's wealth advice service.

$551.3 billion in "advice solutions" as of AUM.
Depending on the degree of assistance, account minimums range from $500,000 to $1 million.
Fees vary depending on the adviser network; 0.80%

Investors Fidelity

One of the biggest financial services firms in the US, Fidelity has been around for more than 75 years. For customers wishing to work with financial experts, the organization provides a few possibilities. Consider Fidelity's phone-based advisors if you're seeking for a basic level of help, such as creating an investment strategy and maintaining focus on your objectives. For a 1.1 percent advisory fee and a minimum investment of $50,000, they will assist you in creating a retirement savings strategy and tax-smart investing strategies to help you achieve your goals.

You will require at least $250,000 in assets and may have to pay annual advice costs of up to 1% if you want your own personal advisor. You'll also have access to a wider selection of services, like estate planning and insurance, at this additional cost.

AUM: Discretionary client assets worth $652,6 billion.

Depending on the degree of assistance, account minimums range from $50,000 to $2 million.

Charges: 0.50 to 1.50 percent

Facet Facet is among the list's most distinctive financial advisory firms since it assesses a flat price based on the intricacy of your financial position rather than an annual fee based on your asset level. Your fee will typically vary from $2,000 to $8,000 each year, and your advisor will be a certified financial planner (CFP) who serves as a fiduciary. Although it may seem like a lot, for investors with $1 million or more in assets, and in some cases even for those with lesser asset levels, it actually turns out to be fairly reasonable.

Working with a dedicated financial advisor who you meet with via video conference is what you can expect. You can get their assistance with a wide range of financial matters, including retirement planning, taxes, home buying, college savings, insurance, estate planning, and more. Anyone can sign up because there are no investment minimums, but those who have already saved a lot of money will benefit from the fees the most.

Discretionary client assets as of AUM: $2.1 billion
Minimum balances: none
Fees: $2000 to $8000 annually
Advisor to Private Clients at J.P.

Although J.P. Morgan is perhaps best known as the biggest bank in the United States, it also provides financial advising services at a competitive price compared to most other industry behemoths. You can collaborate with a group of advisors to create a unique financial plan with J.P. Morgan Personal Advisors. The costs for assets up to $250,000 start at 0.6 percent, and because these advisors are fiduciaries, they will put your interests ahead of their own.

With J.P. Morgan Private Client adviser, you can work directly with a committed adviser in your area for a more individualized experience. You'll receive a customized financial plan and an investment portfolio that are based on your requirements and objectives. Fees for this service begin at 1.45% annually and decrease as your portfolio increases. Depending on how your portfolio is invested, there can be additional costs.

AUM: Discretionary Client Assets of $200.5 billion
Minimum balances vary by account type and range from $20,000 to $120,000.

Fees: 1.95% is the maximum advising charge; additional fees may be assessed.

Jones, Edward

While Edward Jones provides a conventional financial adviser experience, its costs are lower than those of other well-known firms, which frequently exceed 3 percent annually. You can get started with as little as $6,000, but if you want your advisor to manage your portfolio for you, you'll need at least $30,000. Starting at 1.95 percent, fees become less expensive as asset levels increase. For some accounts, there is also a portfolio strategy charge that starts at 0.50 percent and drops to 0.20 percent for assets over $15 million.

With locations in all 50 states, Edward Jones has close to 19,000 financial advisors. The company provides a range of services, including insurance, estate planning, education savings, retirement planning, and more.

AUM: Client discretionary assets valued at $280.4 billion

Depending on the type of account, account minimums range from $6,000 to $600,000.

Program fees begin at 1.50 percent, and additional costs may also apply.

Chapter 9

Achieving Self- and Loved Ones' Protection

Organize your finances.

Organize your finances so you can calculate how much you'll need for daily expenses. To make the transition simpler, gradually cut back on your spending in the years before retiring. Find out if there are any unused pensions, apply for your state pension, and see what other benefits you are eligible for.

2. Gently finish up

Retiring gradually will make the transition easier. You'll be able to grow used to the concept of not working and find other ways to spend your time if you gradually reduce your workload over a number of years. If you can reduce your work hours, ask your employer to do so.

3. Be ready for both ups and downs

It's common to experience moments when you feel a little lost or lonely. Accept that your plans have been momentarily derailed by illness or changes in your relationships and move on to your backup strategy. Be optimistic and discuss any worries with others.

Whether it's picking up a new skill, learning a new language, or gaining a certification, use your leisure time to keep your mind sharp.

4. Consume healthfully

Make sure you consume regular meals, especially if your previous workday eating routine consisted of frequent snacks. Investigate healthy cooking options while you have more time on your hands.

5. Establish a schedule

Continually rising, eating, and retiring at nearly the same times each day may make you feel more normal. Schedule recurring activities including volunteer work, physical activity, and hobbies. This will keep things interesting for you and offer you something to do.

6. Make mental progress

Use your free time to continue to cognitively challenge yourself by learning an instrument, a language, or obtaining a certificate, since research from the government has proven that studying can help seniors maintain their independence.

7. Maintain an active lifestyle

If you haven't previously made exercise a regular part of your life, start by aiming to do at least 150 minutes of moderate-intensity physical activity each week. Consider participating in a charity event to give yourself something to strive for.

8. Make a list

Writing down your goals might serve as a "to do" list to help you stay focused on what you actually want to accomplish. Decide what you can afford to do and set aside time to complete it so you feel a sense of success similar to what you would have experienced at work.

9. Look for social assistance

When you retire, it's typical to feel a little lost because for many individuals, work can play a significant role in their social lives. Join clubs and organizations to fill in the gaps.

10. Conciliate and move on.

Keep your thoughts off of your working days during your retirement. Recognize that you've done all you can in that position, and then concentrate on the problem ahead. You still have a lot of work to do.

11. Get a physical examination

Now is the ideal time to get your free midlife MOT because prevention is always preferable to treatment. Heart disease, stroke, diabetes, kidney disease, and some forms of dementia are among the conditions that the NHS Health Check program attempts to help people avoid.

Every person between the ages of 40 and 74, who has not yet been diagnosed with one of these conditions or has certain risk factors, will be invited once every five years to have a checkup to assess their risk of these age-related illnesses and will be given support and advice to help them reduce or manage that risk.

You can request a checkup from your doctor if you fall into this category but haven't had one in the previous five years.

12. Maintain contact with your coworkers.

You don't necessarily have to stop communicating with the friends you established at work just because you're retiring. Why not arrange for frequent catch-ups? Alternatively, you could choose to spend part of your newfound free time visiting with long-lost acquaintances.

Find a reason to get everyone together if you enjoy planning parties, and then have fun creating the ideal garden or dinner party, anniversary celebration, or other special occasion. Through our "Give in Celebration" funding, you might even raise money for our life-saving work concurrently.

13. Reward yourself

You deserve some "me time" after years of tough effort. Make time in your calendar for a well-deserved treat, whether it's a city vacation, a spa day, or a modest pleasure like going to the movies or dining out.

14. Become more mindful.

In the past ten years, using mindfulness as a technique to combat stress, anxiety, and depression has grown in popularity more than ever.

Exercise and getting some fresh air instantly improve your mood. They also help you stay healthy.

Research, including a 2009 research from Goethe University in Germany, has demonstrated that meditation enhances the hippocampus, a region of the brain critical for remembering, and slows the deterioration of brain regions necessary for maintaining attention.

There are no set rules for how often to practice meditation for best results, but a few studies indicate that even just 10 to 20 minutes of mindfulness practice each day—if people persist with it—can be helpful.

15. Volunteer in your community

Have you considered volunteering? You might appreciate getting involved with a local youth club, animal shelter, environmental group, or senior support group.

Numerous organizations, including the BHF of course, would appreciate assistance. We give customers the option to volunteer in our stores, at a furniture or electronics store, during fundraisers, and at a wide range of events.

16. Connect to nature

Exercise and access to the great outdoors are both essential to sustaining your wellbeing. Why not include a stroll around some nearby parks or in the woods in your regular routine? This is the best way to fulfill the weekly minimum physical activity recommendation of 150 minutes.

17. Take more trips

Ever wanted to take a globe cruise, a wine tasting tour of Italy, or a straightforward camping trip through the Welsh valleys? Depending on your health and financial constraints, you can now make your long-held plans a reality.

If longer travels are not feasible, small holidays or even days out to new locations could be a suitable option.

18. Get a new animal.

Could you provide a new home for a stray cat or dog? Our animal companions benefit our health and happiness, according to research.

People who own dogs tend to be happier, more trustworthy, and less lonely than those who do not, claims pet researcher Allen R. McConnell, a professor of psychology at Miami University. They also go to the doctor less frequently for smaller issues.

According to Prof. McConnell, one explanation for this could be the sense of community and purpose your pet provides for you. You perceive a better sense of control over your life.

19. Push the limits.

Doing something unusual can be a welcome shift because it's simple to become stagnant, both in terms of your health and in general. Some people have discovered that making small adjustments to their routine, such as trying a new dish, going to a different hairdresser, or enrolling in an exercise class, can give them a newfound sense of enthusiasm for life.

20. embark on a new undertaking

Finally, you have the opportunity to tackle all the tasks you have been meaning to complete but have put off. You can now carry out all of your long-held goals, including mapping your family tree and creating a shed or a vegetable garden.